JR. GRAPHIC GHOST STORIES

AMITYVILLE

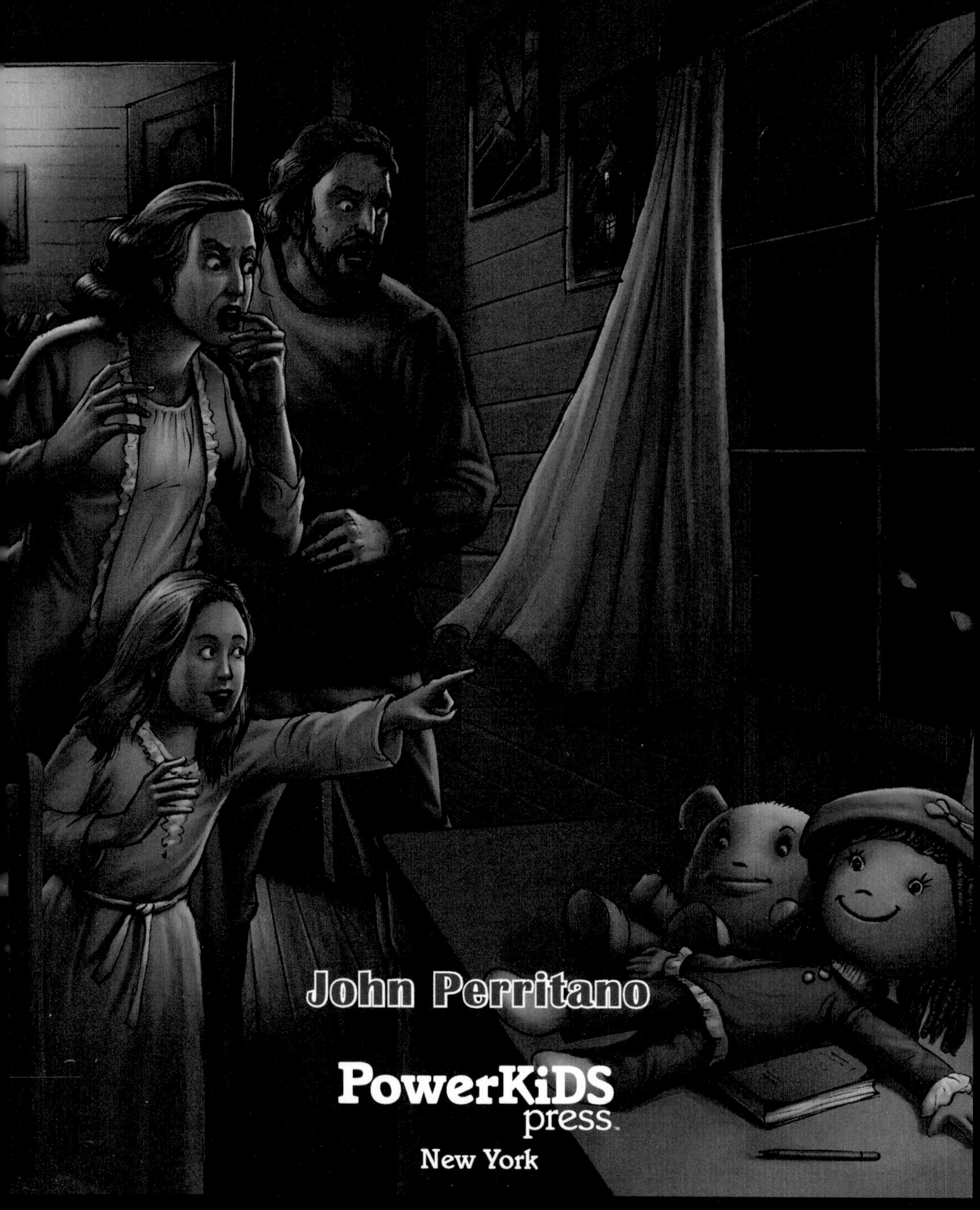

John Perritano

PowerKiDS press
New York

Published in 2015 by The Rosen Publishing Group, Inc.
29 East 21st Street, New York, NY 10010

First Edition

Editor: Joanne Randolph
Book Design: Contentra Technologies
Illustrations: Contentra Technologies

Publisher's Cataloging Data

Perritano, John.
Amityville / by John Perritano. — 1st ed.
        p. cm. — (Jr. graphic ghost stories)
Includes an index.
ISBN: 978-1-4777-7121-1 (Library Binding)
ISBN: 978-1-4777-7122-8 (Paperback)
ISBN: 978-1-4777-7123-5 (6-pack)
1. Ghosts—Juvenile literature. 2. Haunted houses—Juvenile literature.
I. Title.
BF1461.P47 2015
398

Manufactured in the United States of America

CPSIA Compliance Information: Batch #WS14PK2: For Further Information contact Rosen Publishing, New York, New York at 1-800-237-9932

Contents

Introduction

This story is based on real events that occurred in Amityville, New York. A very **troubled** young man killed his family after he thought he heard voices telling him to do so. He was brought to justice and sentenced to prison for the murders. The family who bought the house after these events experienced some very odd **occurrences**. They believed the house was haunted by the ghosts of the murdered family.

Main Characters

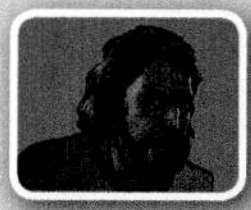

George Lutz (1947–2006) A land surveyor. In 1975, George moved his wife and three children into what would later become the most famous haunted house in America, 112 Ocean Avenue, Amityville, New York.

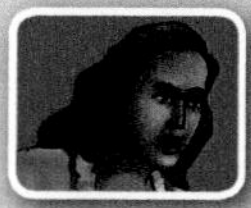

Kathy Lutz (1946–2004) George Lutz's wife. Soon after moving to Amityville, strange things began to happen to Kathy. She would smell a cheap perfume and feel the **sensation** of a woman **embracing** her from behind.

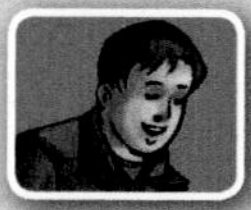

Danny Lutz (b. 1965) Danny, 10 years old at the time, has always **maintained** that the haunting in Amityville was real.

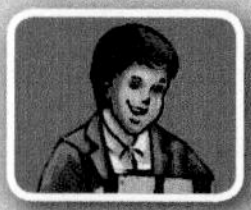

Christopher Lutz (b. 1968) Chris, 7 years old at the time of the haunting, shared a room with Danny.

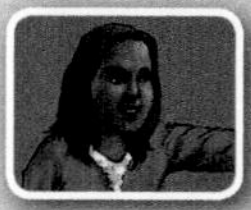

Melissa "Missy" Lutz (b. 1970) Missy, 5 at the time of the haunting, claimed to have seen a pig named Jodie. She described the pig as an angel.

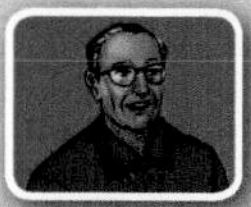

Father Mancuso (d. 1980s) Father Ralph J. Pecoraro, known in this story as Father Mancuso, visited the house on the day the Lutzes moved in, only to be told by a voice to "get out." The priest would later experience many health problems, which he claimed were caused by the Amityville ghosts.

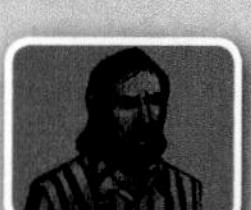

Ronald "Butch" DeFeo Jr. (b. 1951) He killed his family while they were sleeping. DeFeo claimed voices told him to shoot his parents, brothers, and sisters. He was tried and found guilty of the murders.

The Ghosts of Amityville

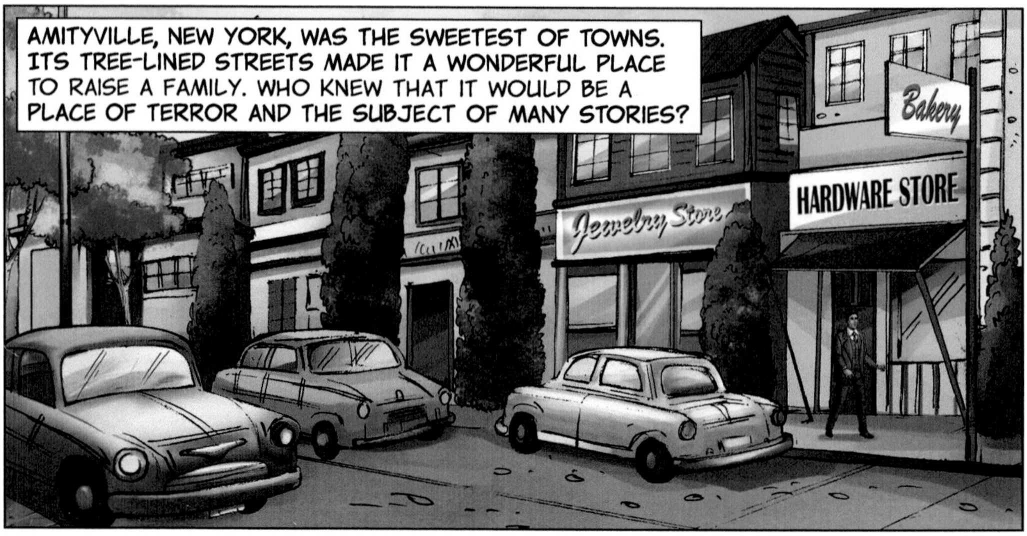
AMITYVILLE, NEW YORK, WAS THE SWEETEST OF TOWNS. ITS TREE-LINED STREETS MADE IT A WONDERFUL PLACE TO RAISE A FAMILY. WHO KNEW THAT IT WOULD BE A PLACE OF TERROR AND THE SUBJECT OF MANY STORIES?
Bakery
Jewelry Store
HARDWARE STORE

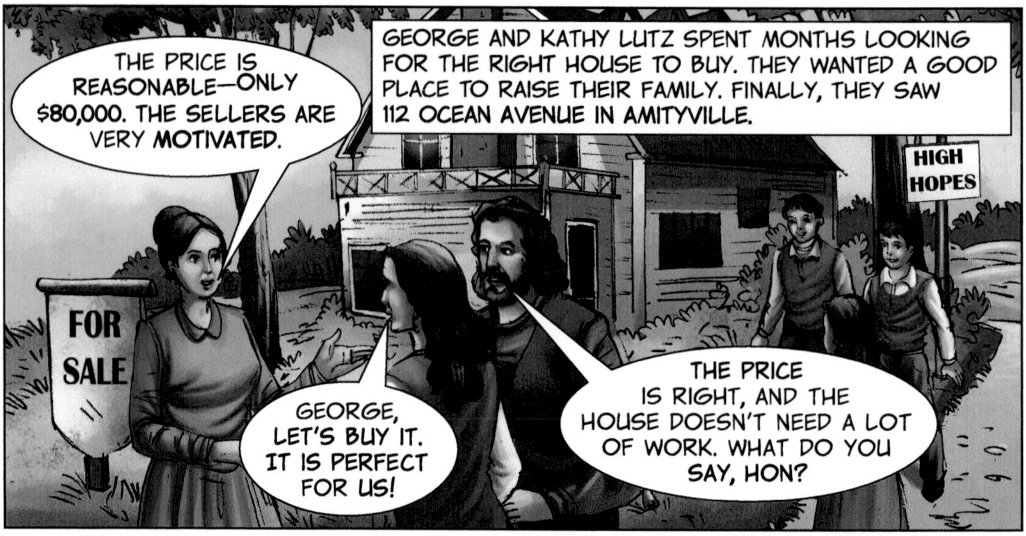
GEORGE AND KATHY LUTZ SPENT MONTHS LOOKING FOR THE RIGHT HOUSE TO BUY. THEY WANTED A GOOD PLACE TO RAISE THEIR FAMILY. FINALLY, THEY SAW 112 OCEAN AVENUE IN AMITYVILLE.
THE PRICE IS REASONABLE—ONLY $80,000. THE SELLERS ARE VERY MOTIVATED.
HIGH HOPES
FOR SALE
THE PRICE IS RIGHT, AND THE HOUSE DOESN'T NEED A LOT OF WORK. WHAT DO YOU SAY, HON?
GEORGE, LET'S BUY IT. IT IS PERFECT FOR US!

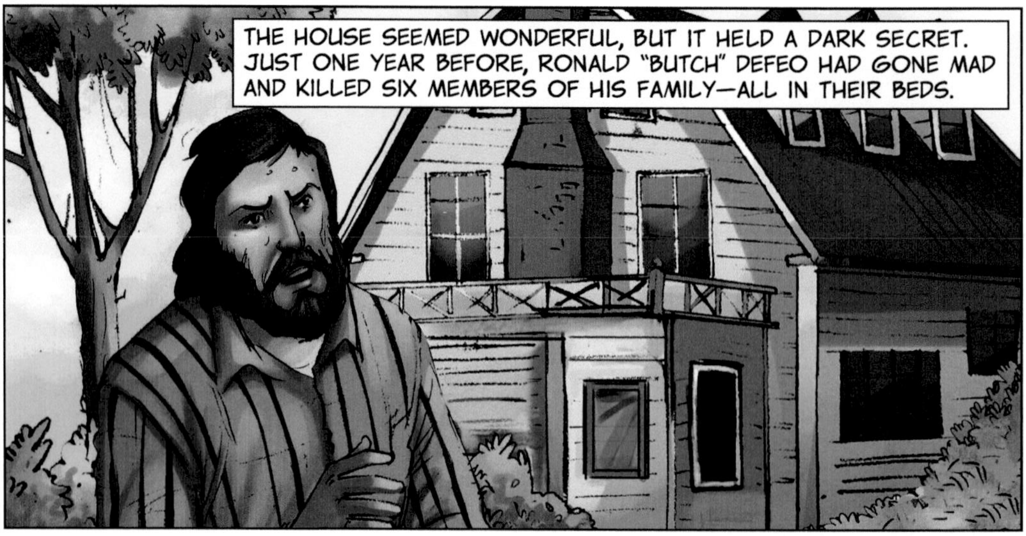
THE HOUSE SEEMED WONDERFUL, BUT IT HELD A DARK SECRET. JUST ONE YEAR BEFORE, RONALD "BUTCH" DEFEO HAD GONE MAD AND KILLED SIX MEMBERS OF HIS FAMILY—ALL IN THEIR BEDS.

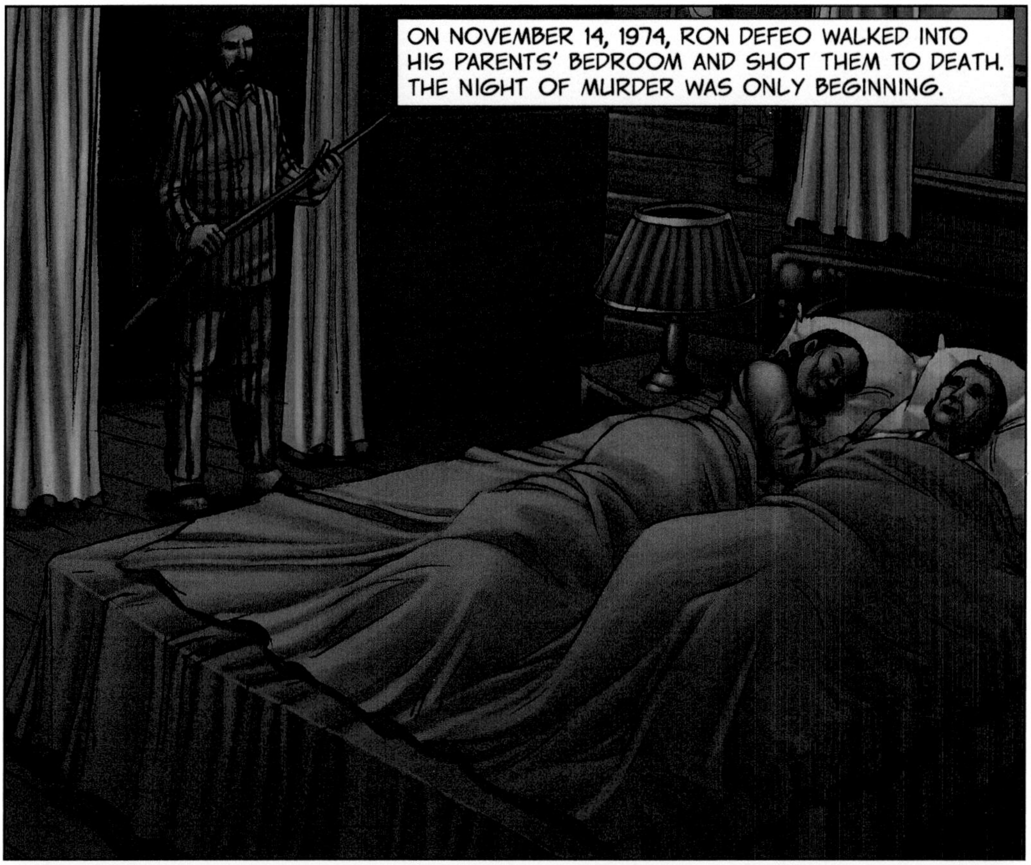
ON NOVEMBER 14, 1974, RON DEFEO WALKED INTO HIS PARENTS' BEDROOM AND SHOT THEM TO DEATH. THE NIGHT OF MURDER WAS ONLY BEGINNING.

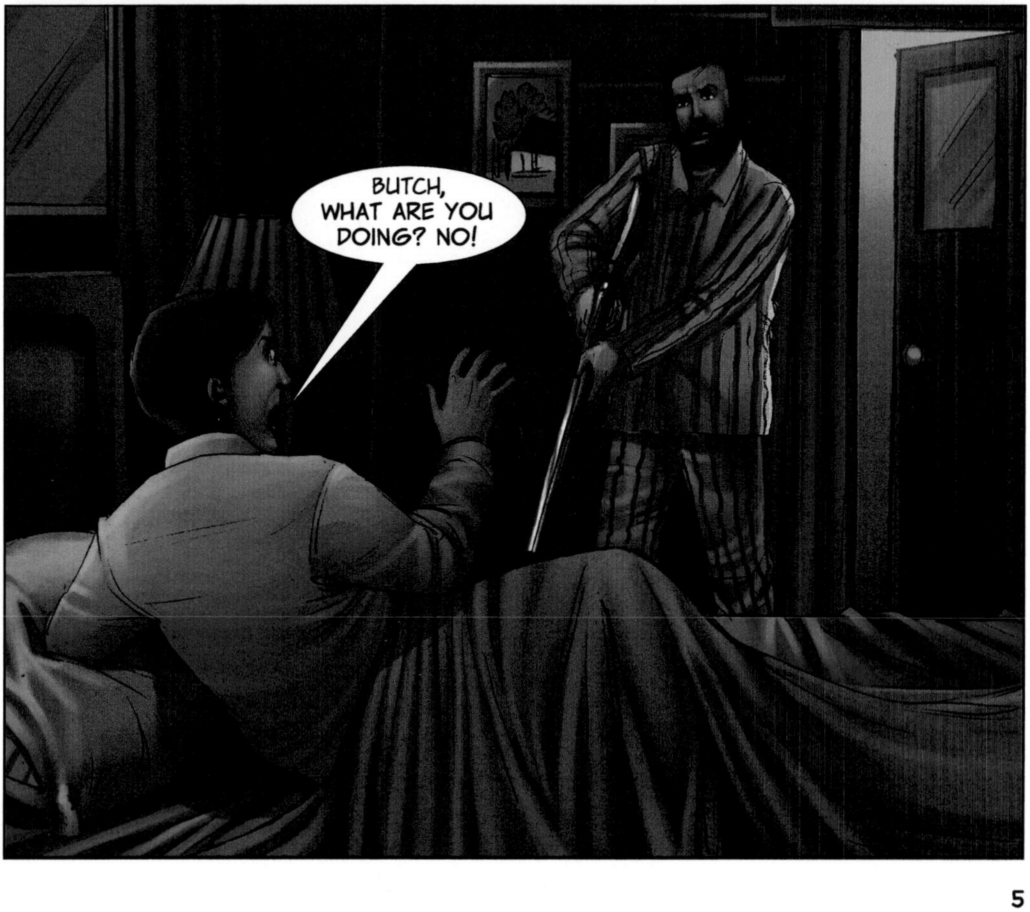
BUTCH, WHAT ARE YOU DOING? NO!

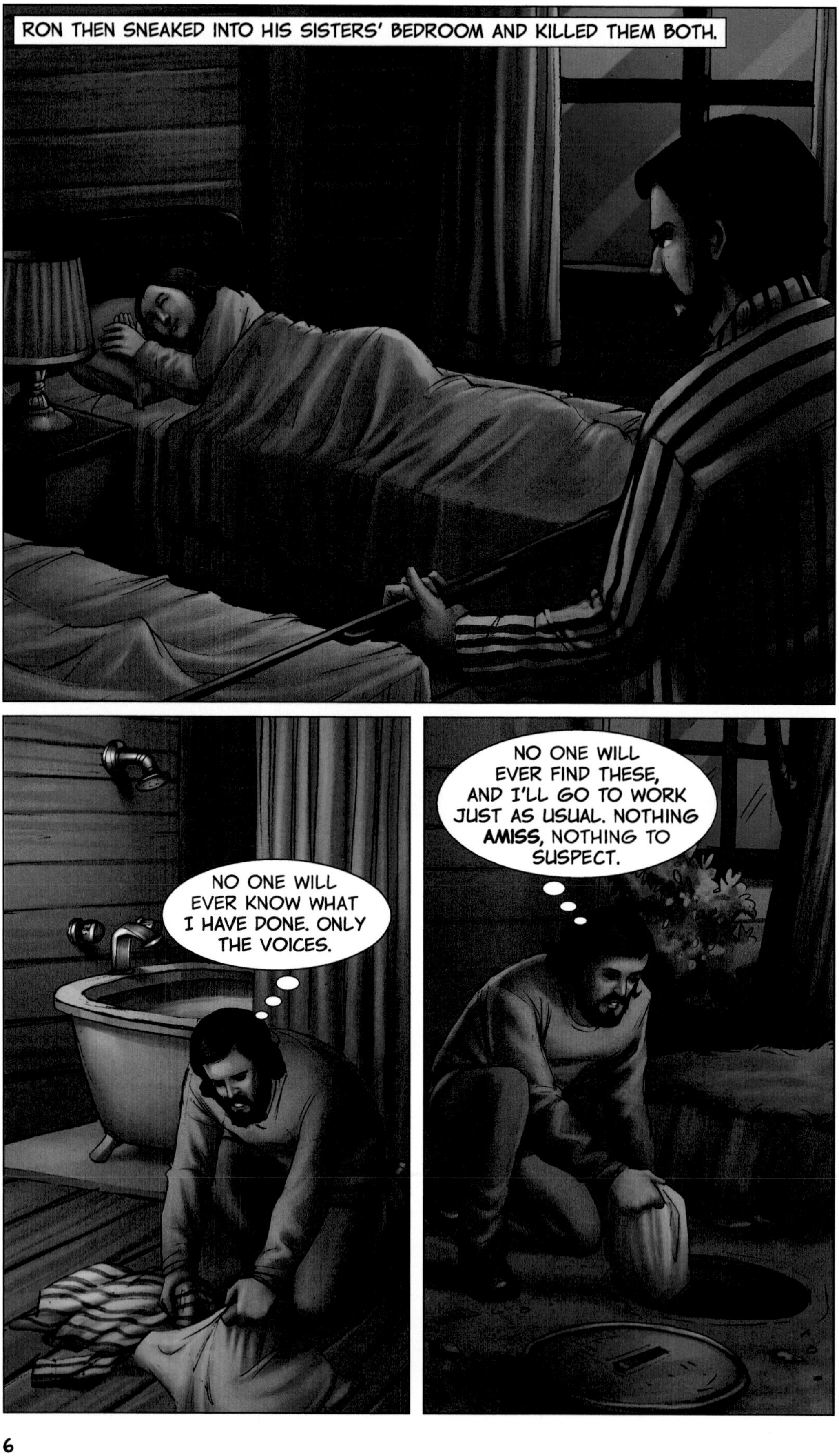
RON THEN SNEAKED INTO HIS SISTERS' BEDROOM AND KILLED THEM BOTH.
NO ONE WILL EVER KNOW WHAT I HAVE DONE. ONLY THE VOICES.
NO ONE WILL EVER FIND THESE, AND I'LL GO TO WORK JUST AS USUAL. NOTHING **AMISS,** NOTHING TO SUSPECT.

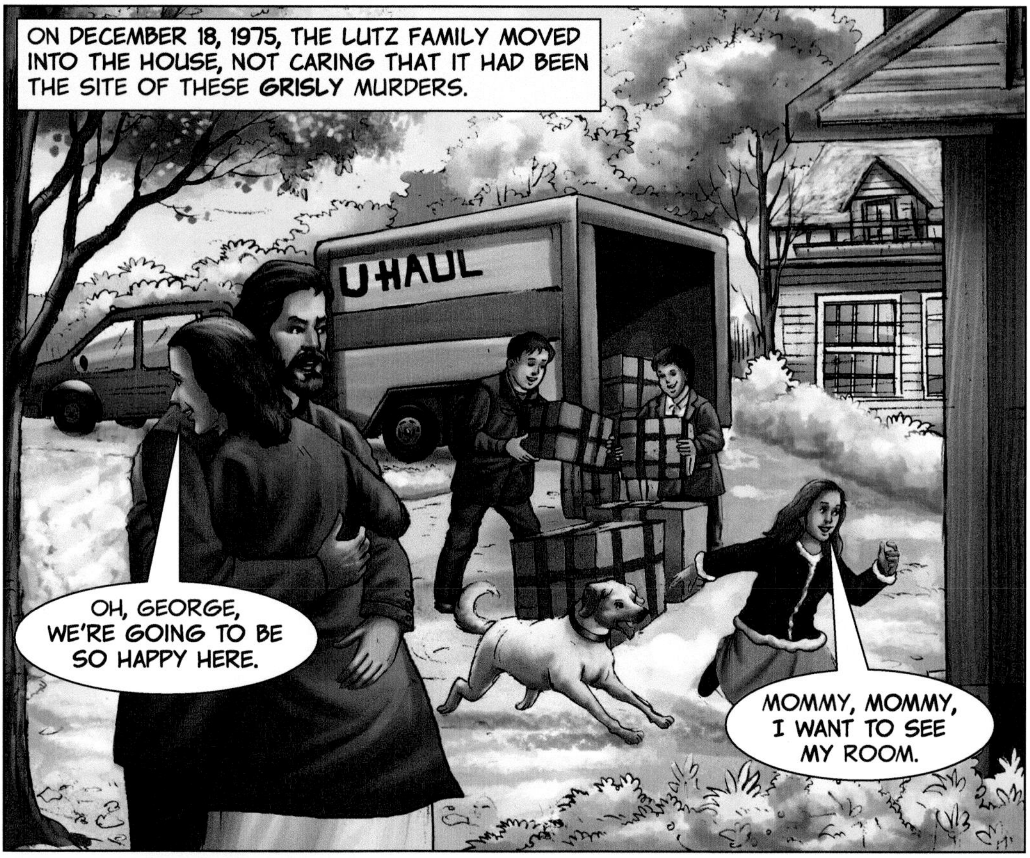
ON DECEMBER 18, 1975, THE LUTZ FAMILY MOVED INTO THE HOUSE, NOT CARING THAT IT HAD BEEN THE SITE OF THESE GRISLY MURDERS.
U-HAUL
OH, GEORGE, WE'RE GOING TO BE SO HAPPY HERE.
MOMMY, MOMMY, I WANT TO SEE MY ROOM.

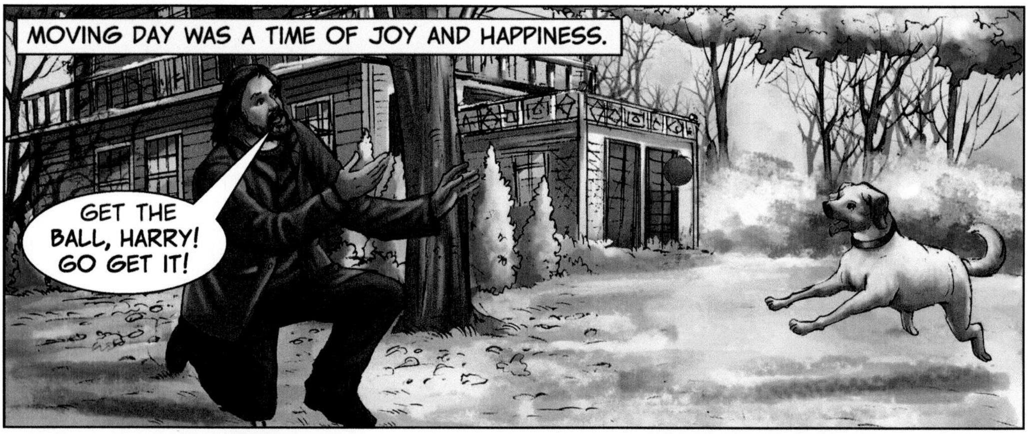
MOVING DAY WAS A TIME OF JOY AND HAPPINESS.
GET THE BALL, HARRY! GO GET IT!

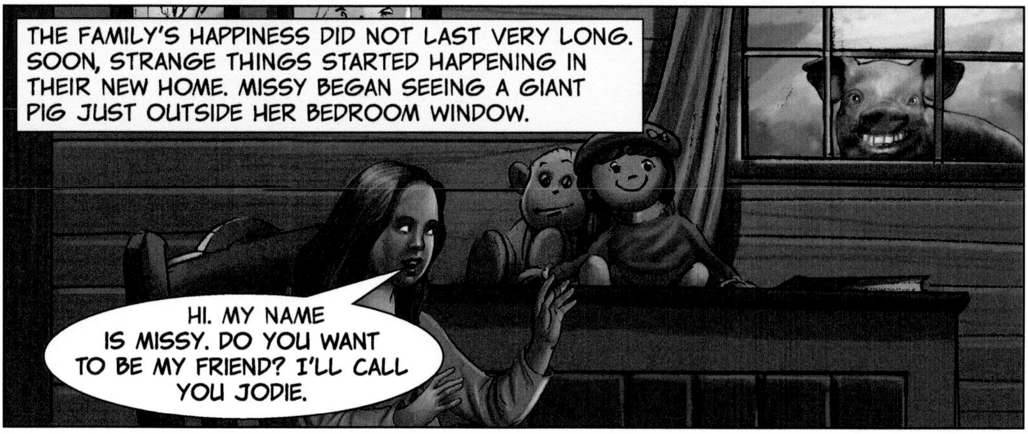
THE FAMILY'S HAPPINESS DID NOT LAST VERY LONG. SOON, STRANGE THINGS STARTED HAPPENING IN THEIR NEW HOME. MISSY BEGAN SEEING A GIANT PIG JUST OUTSIDE HER BEDROOM WINDOW.
HI. MY NAME IS MISSY. DO YOU WANT TO BE MY FRIEND? I'LL CALL YOU JODIE.

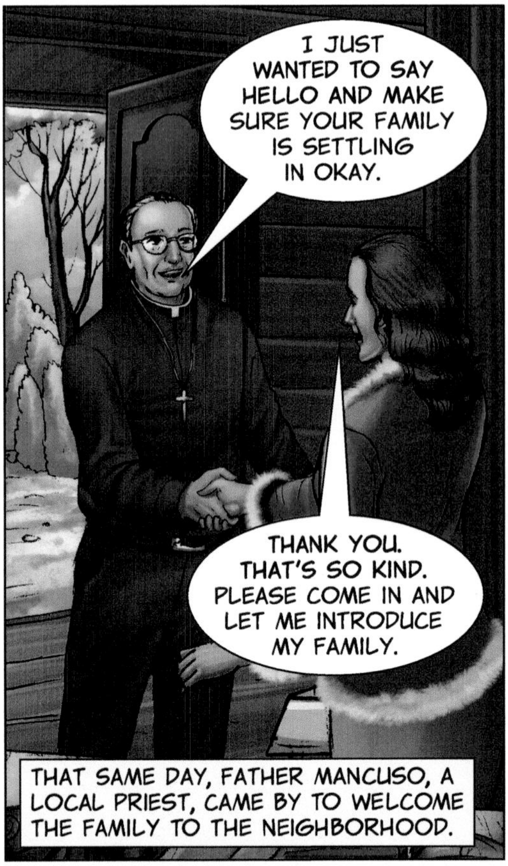
I JUST WANTED TO SAY HELLO AND MAKE SURE YOUR FAMILY IS SETTLING IN OKAY.
THANK YOU. THAT'S SO KIND. PLEASE COME IN AND LET ME INTRODUCE MY FAMILY.
THAT SAME DAY, FATHER MANCUSO, A LOCAL PRIEST, CAME BY TO WELCOME THE FAMILY TO THE NEIGHBORHOOD.

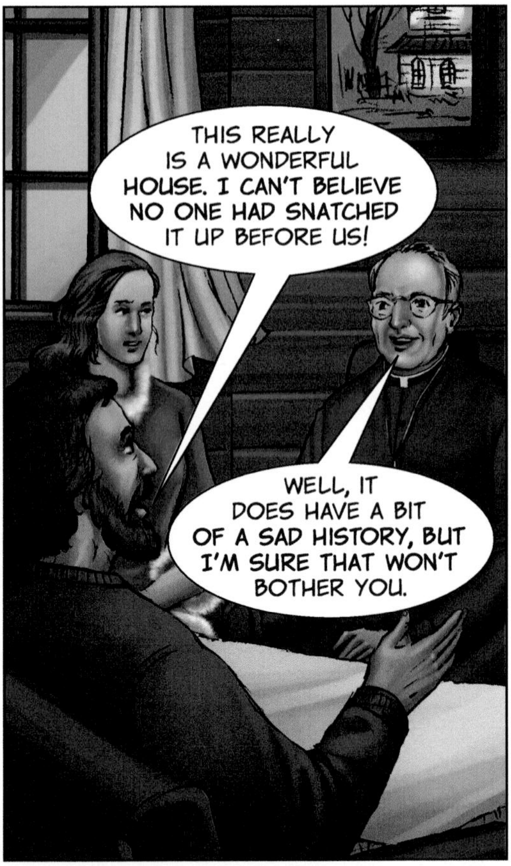
THIS REALLY IS A WONDERFUL HOUSE. I CAN'T BELIEVE NO ONE HAD SNATCHED IT UP BEFORE US!
WELL, IT DOES HAVE A BIT OF A SAD HISTORY, BUT I'M SURE THAT WON'T BOTHER YOU.

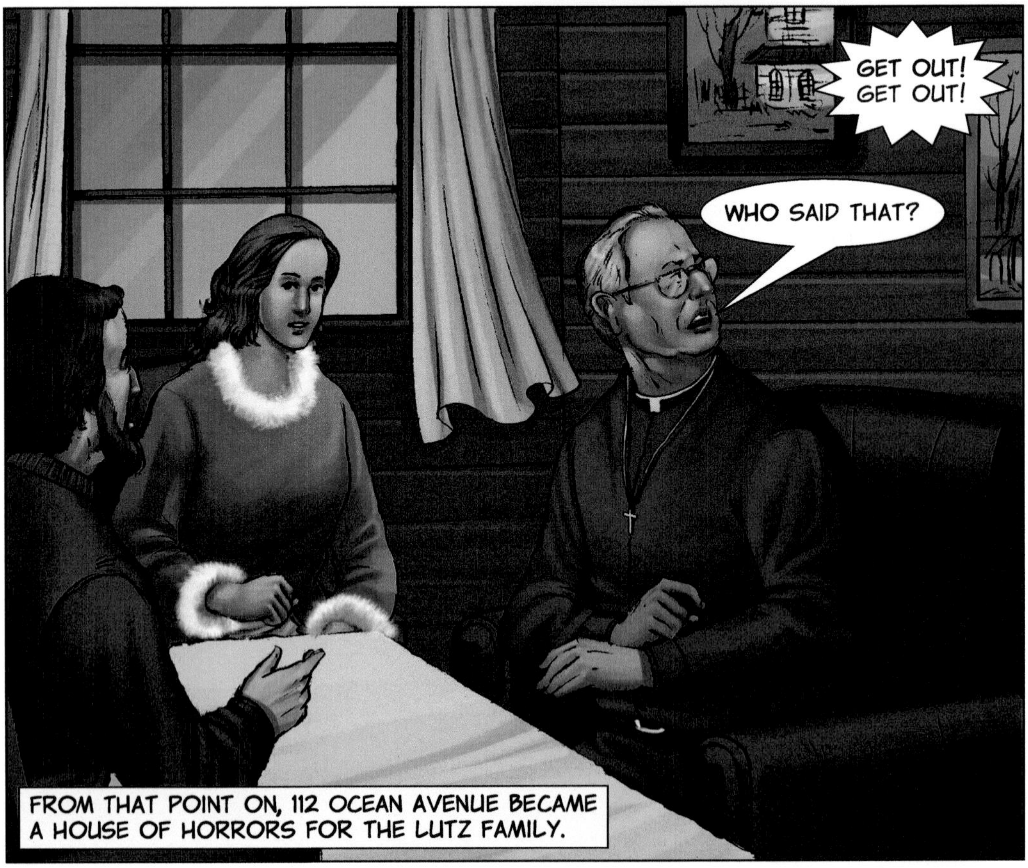
GET OUT! GET OUT!
WHO SAID THAT?
FROM THAT POINT ON, 112 OCEAN AVENUE BECAME A HOUSE OF HORRORS FOR THE LUTZ FAMILY.

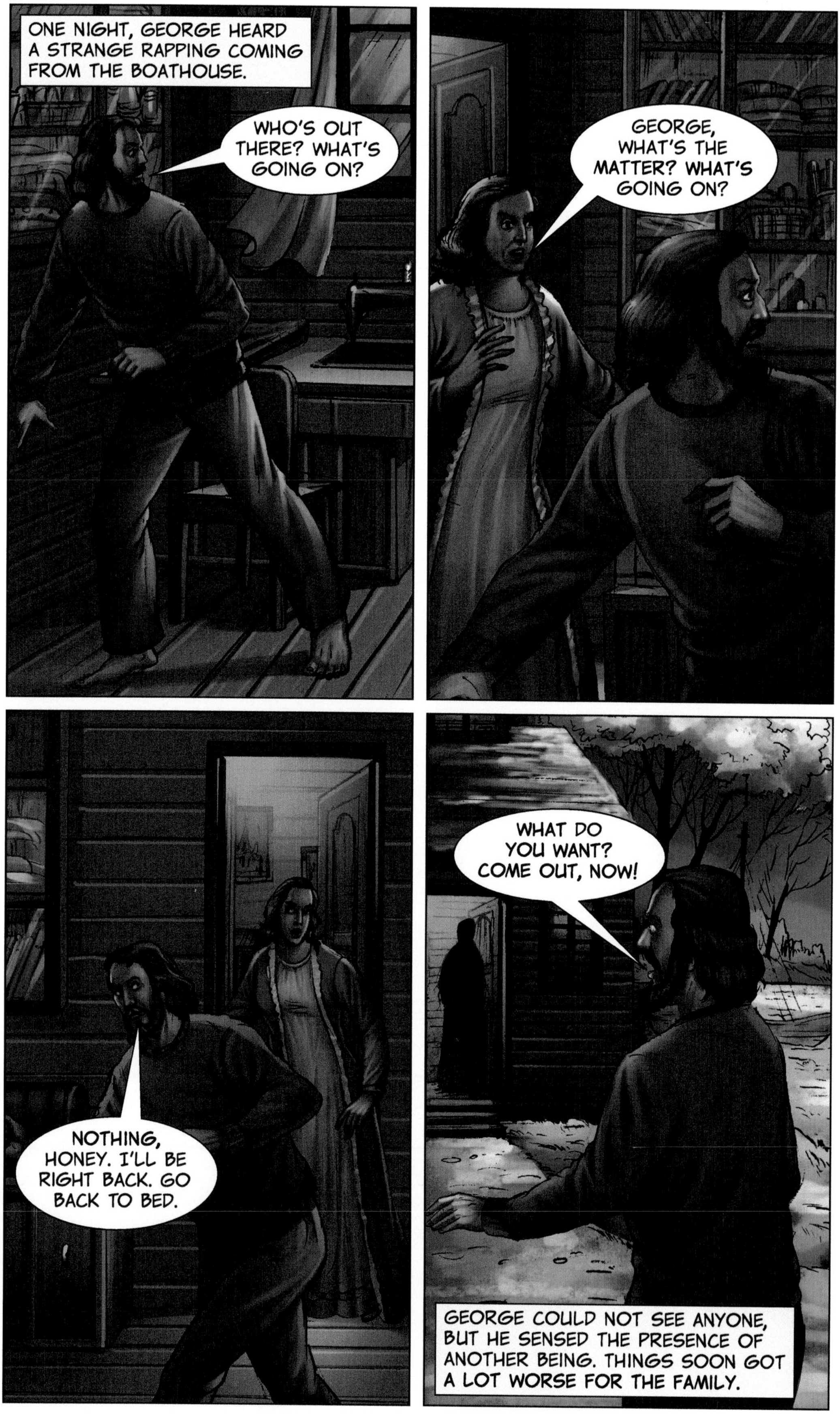
ONE NIGHT, GEORGE HEARD A STRANGE RAPPING COMING FROM THE BOATHOUSE.
WHO'S OUT THERE? WHAT'S GOING ON?
GEORGE, WHAT'S THE MATTER? WHAT'S GOING ON?
NOTHING, HONEY. I'LL BE RIGHT BACK. GO BACK TO BED.
WHAT DO YOU WANT? COME OUT, NOW!
GEORGE COULD NOT SEE ANYONE, BUT HE SENSED THE PRESENCE OF ANOTHER BEING. THINGS SOON GOT A LOT WORSE FOR THE FAMILY.

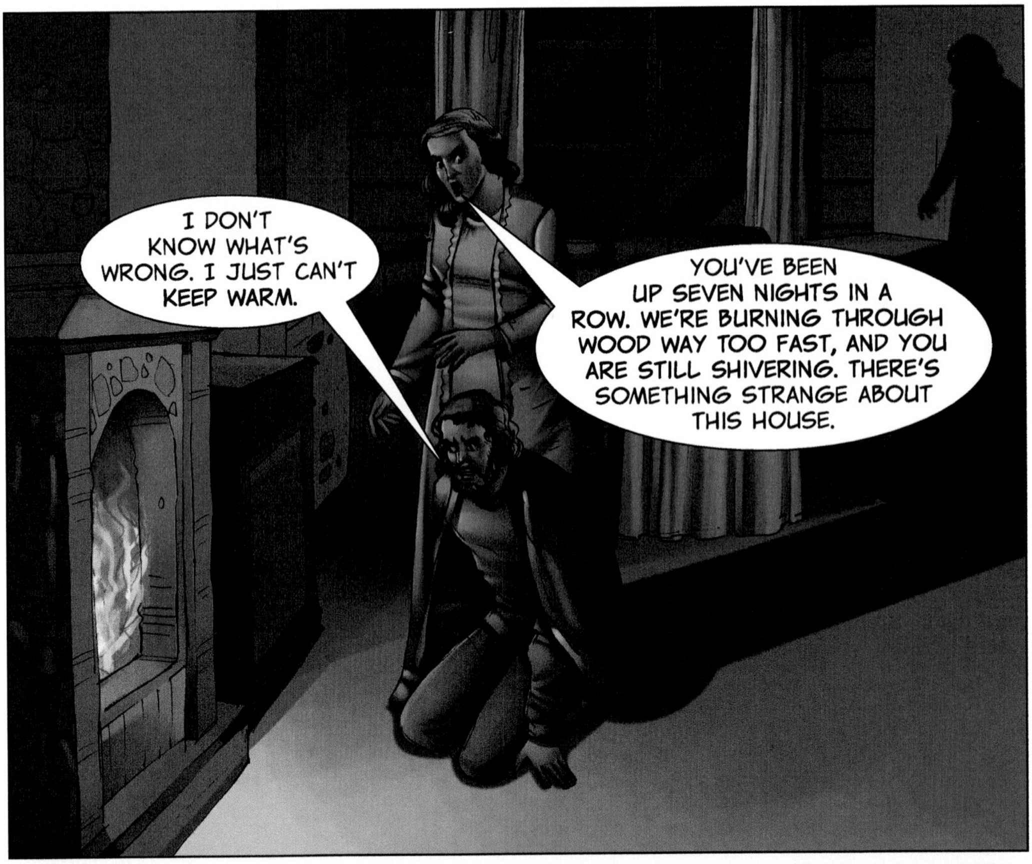
I DON'T KNOW WHAT'S WRONG. I JUST CAN'T KEEP WARM.
YOU'VE BEEN UP SEVEN NIGHTS IN A ROW. WE'RE BURNING THROUGH WOOD WAY TOO FAST, AND YOU ARE STILL SHIVERING. THERE'S SOMETHING STRANGE ABOUT THIS HOUSE.

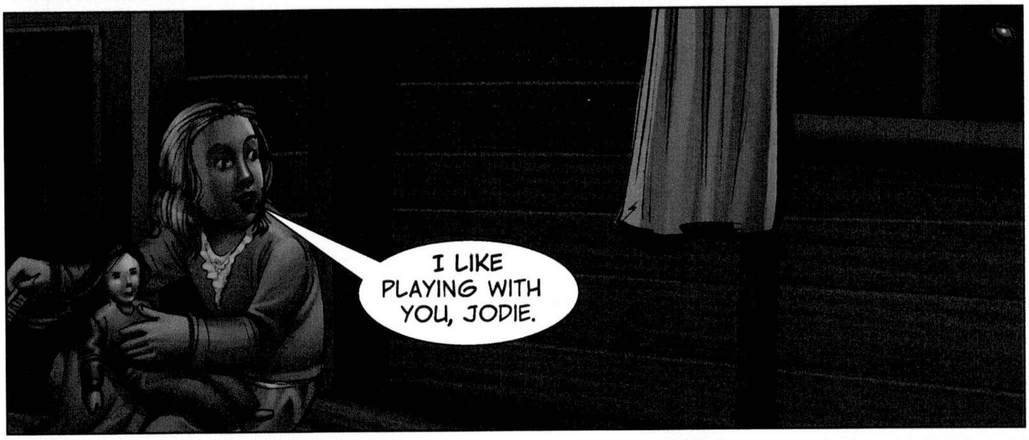
I LIKE PLAYING WITH YOU, JODIE.

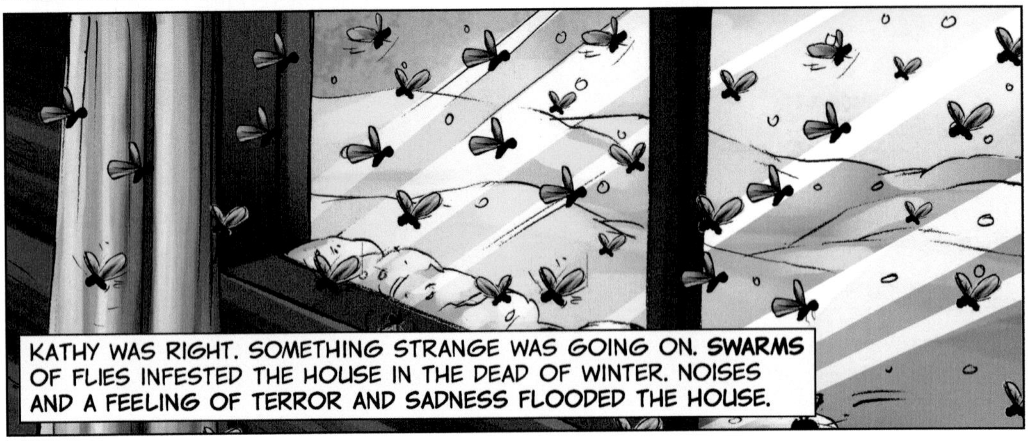
KATHY WAS RIGHT. SOMETHING STRANGE WAS GOING ON. **SWARMS** OF FLIES INFESTED THE HOUSE IN THE DEAD OF WINTER. NOISES AND A FEELING OF TERROR AND SADNESS FLOODED THE HOUSE.

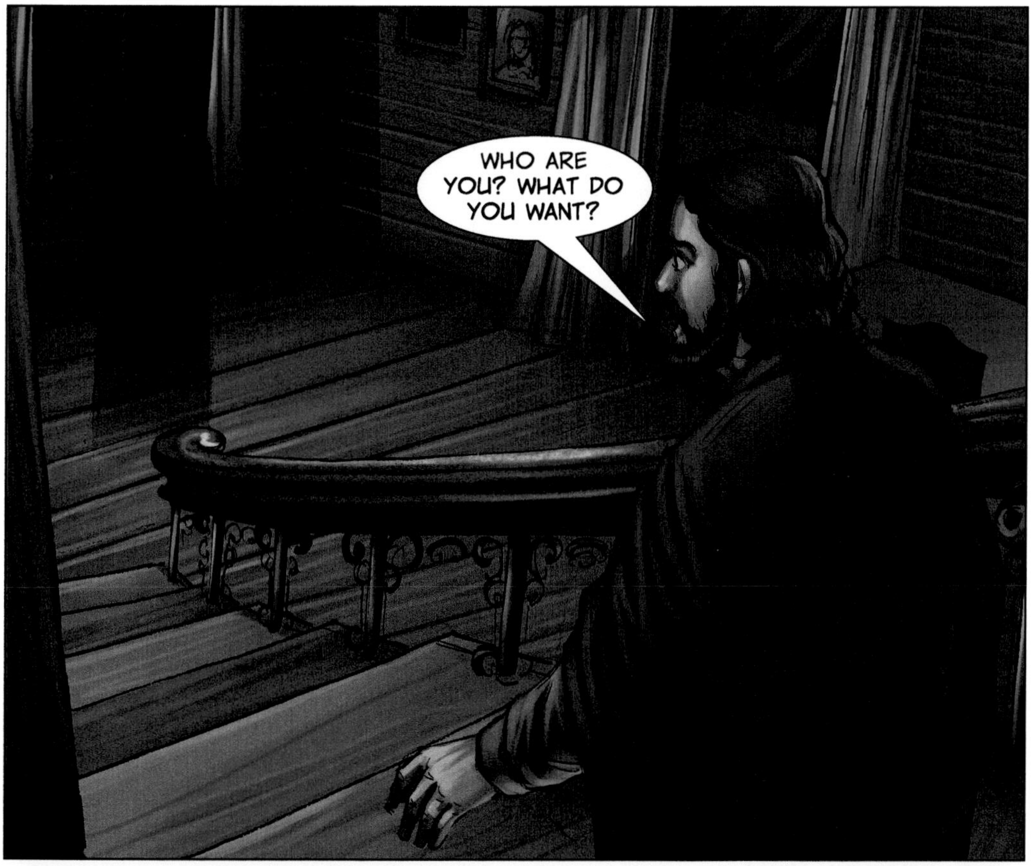
WHO ARE YOU? WHAT DO YOU WANT?

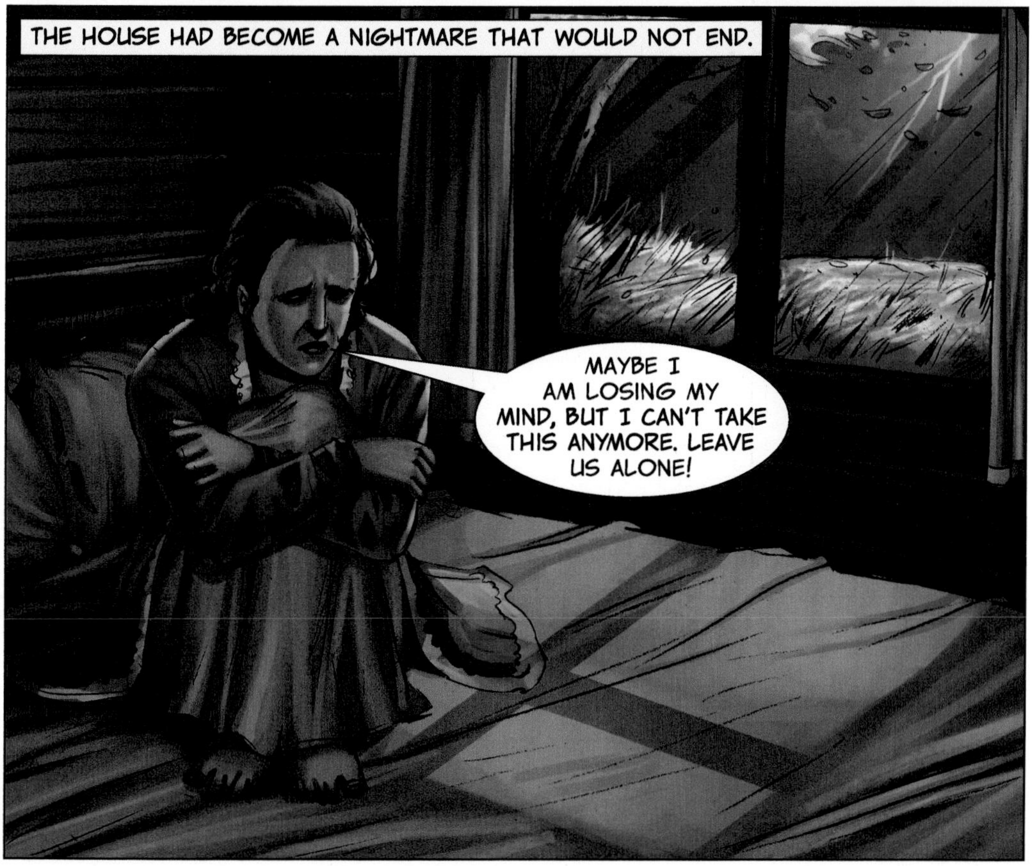
THE HOUSE HAD BECOME A NIGHTMARE THAT WOULD NOT END.
MAYBE I AM LOSING MY MIND, BUT I CAN'T TAKE THIS ANYMORE. LEAVE US ALONE!

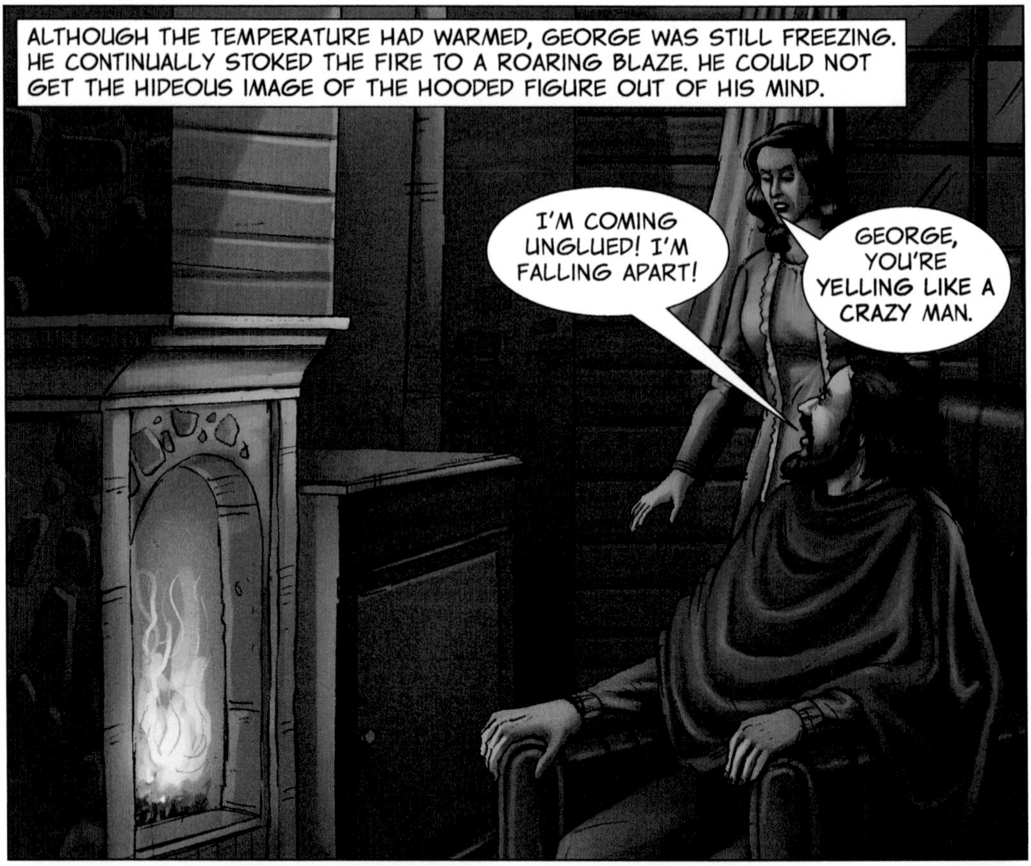
ALTHOUGH THE TEMPERATURE HAD WARMED, GEORGE WAS STILL FREEZING. HE CONTINUALLY STOKED THE FIRE TO A ROARING BLAZE. HE COULD NOT GET THE HIDEOUS IMAGE OF THE HOODED FIGURE OUT OF HIS MIND.
I'M COMING UNGLUED! I'M FALLING APART!
GEORGE, YOU'RE YELLING LIKE A CRAZY MAN.

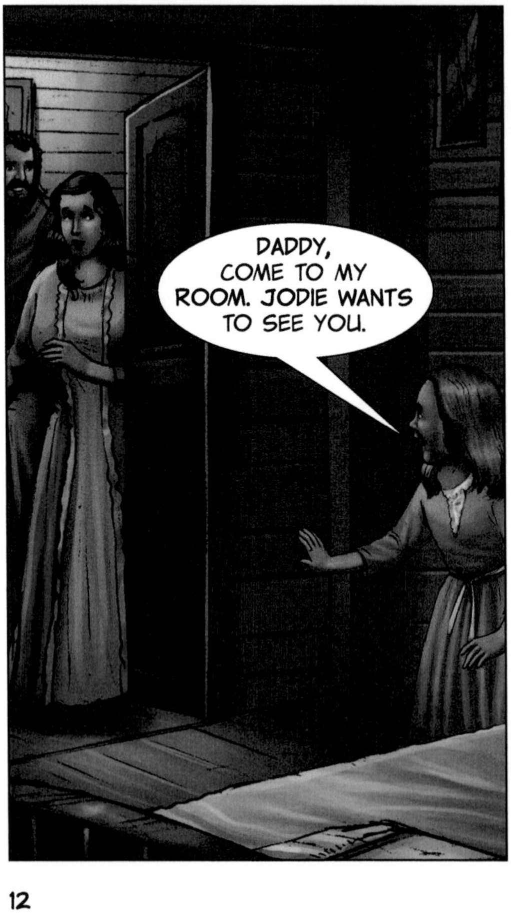
DADDY, COME TO MY ROOM. JODIE WANTS TO SEE YOU.

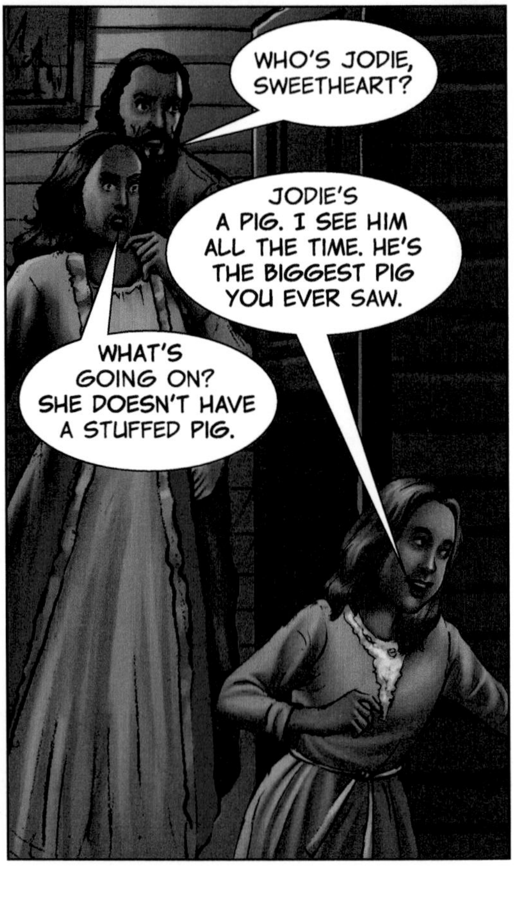
WHO'S JODIE, SWEETHEART?
JODIE'S A PIG. I SEE HIM ALL THE TIME. HE'S THE BIGGEST PIG YOU EVER SAW.
WHAT'S GOING ON? SHE DOESN'T HAVE A STUFFED PIG.

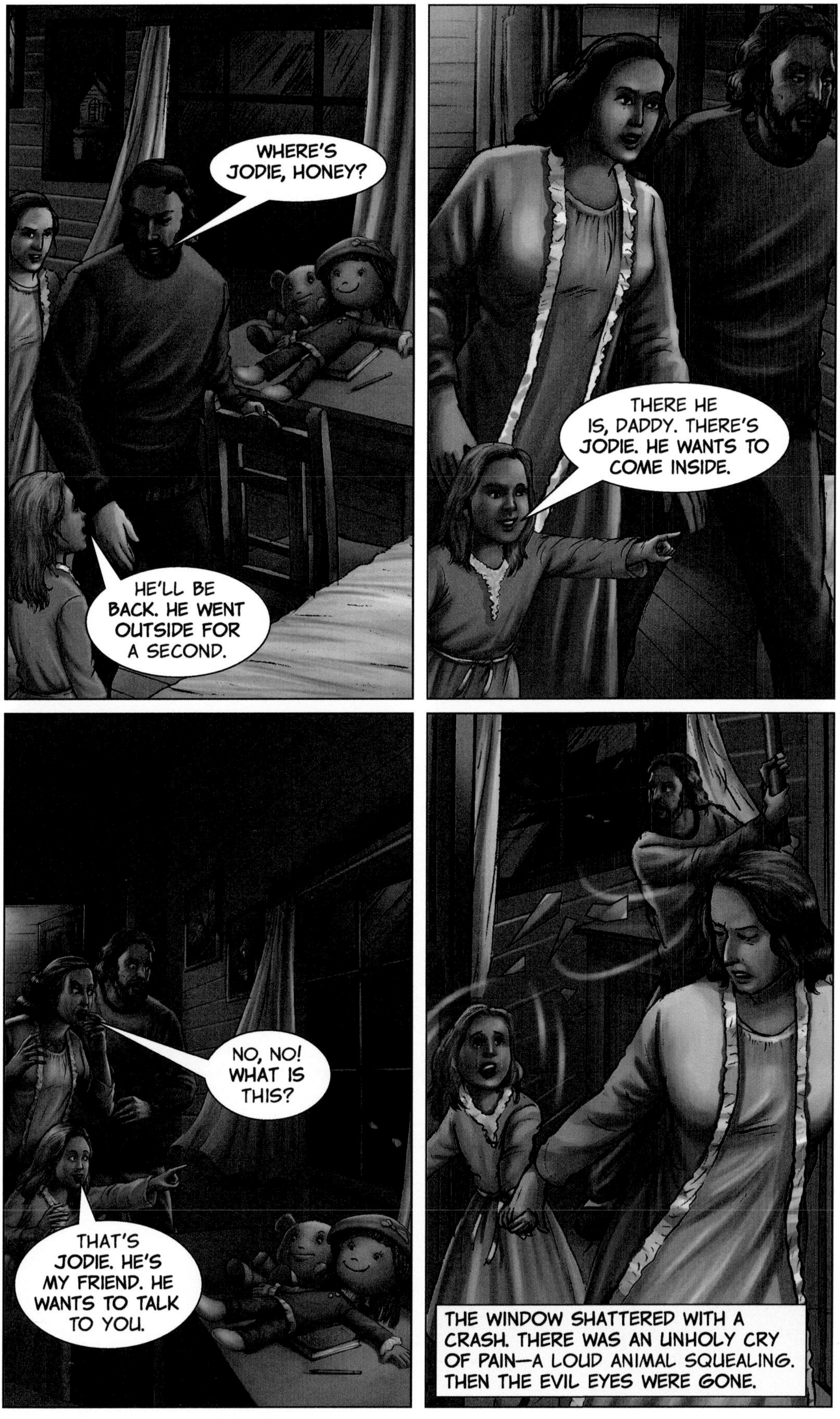
WHERE'S JODIE, HONEY?
HE'LL BE BACK. HE WENT OUTSIDE FOR A SECOND.
THERE HE IS, DADDY. THERE'S JODIE. HE WANTS TO COME INSIDE.
NO, NO! WHAT IS THIS?
THAT'S JODIE. HE'S MY FRIEND. HE WANTS TO TALK TO YOU.
THE WINDOW SHATTERED WITH A CRASH. THERE WAS AN UNHOLY CRY OF PAIN—A LOUD ANIMAL SQUEALING. THEN THE EVIL EYES WERE GONE.

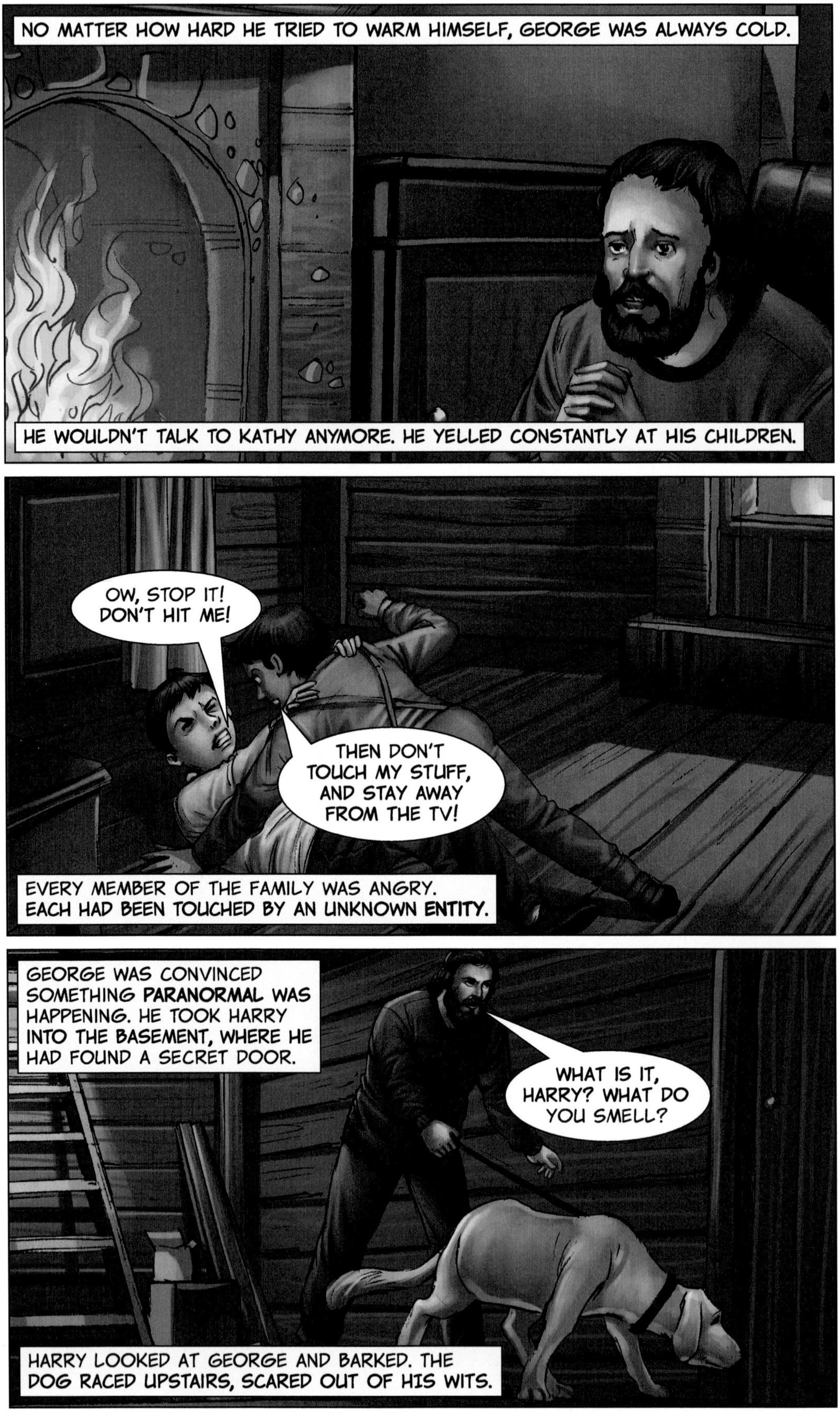
NO MATTER HOW HARD HE TRIED TO WARM HIMSELF, GEORGE WAS ALWAYS COLD.
HE WOULDN'T TALK TO KATHY ANYMORE. HE YELLED CONSTANTLY AT HIS CHILDREN.
OW, STOP IT! DON'T HIT ME!
THEN DON'T TOUCH MY STUFF, AND STAY AWAY FROM THE TV!
EVERY MEMBER OF THE FAMILY WAS ANGRY. EACH HAD BEEN TOUCHED BY AN UNKNOWN **ENTITY**.
GEORGE WAS CONVINCED SOMETHING **PARANORMAL** WAS HAPPENING. HE TOOK HARRY INTO THE **BASEMENT**, WHERE HE HAD FOUND A SECRET DOOR.
WHAT IS IT, HARRY? WHAT DO YOU SMELL?
HARRY LOOKED AT GEORGE AND BARKED. THE DOG RACED UPSTAIRS, SCARED OUT OF HIS WITS.

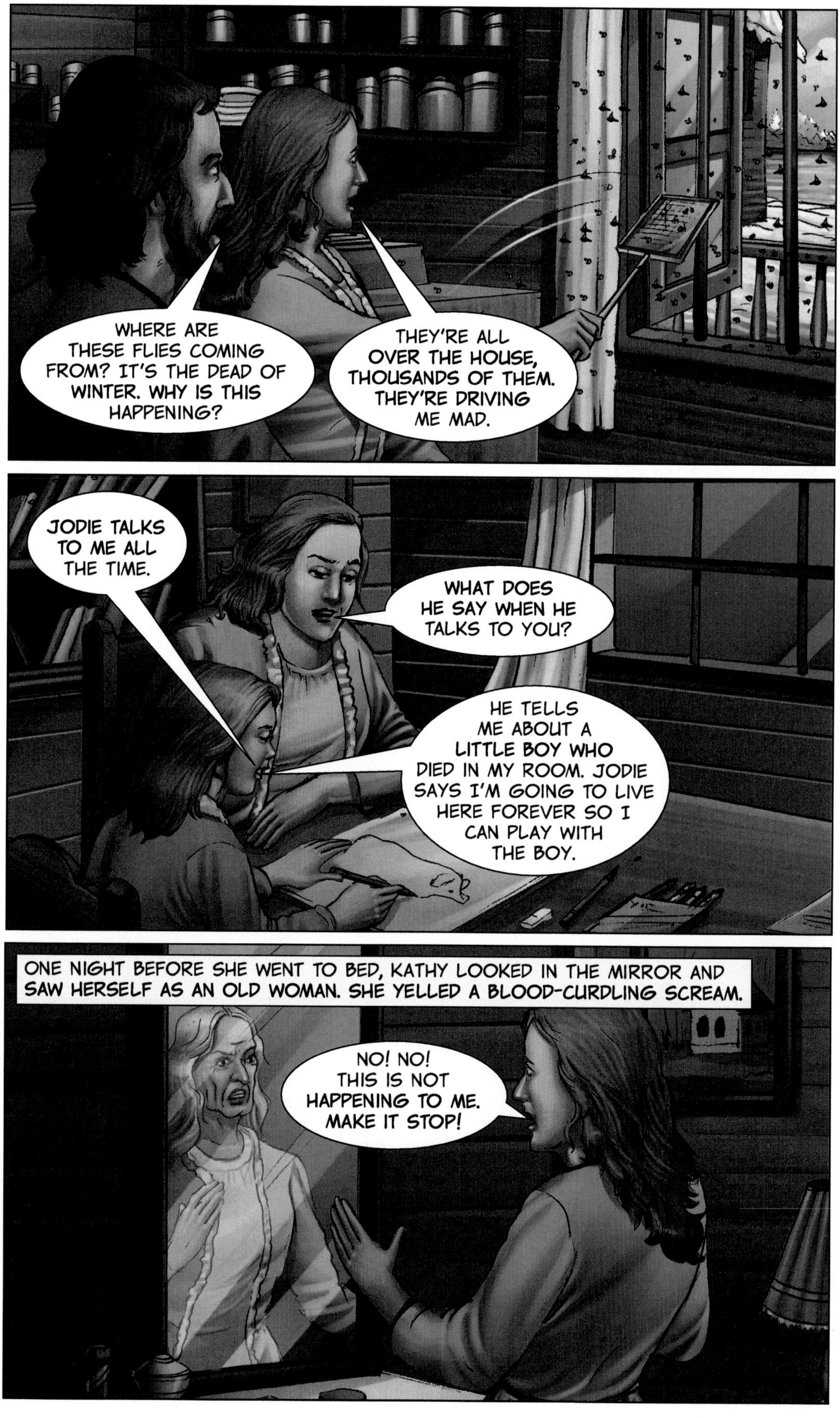
WHERE ARE THESE FLIES COMING FROM? IT'S THE DEAD OF WINTER. WHY IS THIS HAPPENING?
THEY'RE ALL OVER THE HOUSE, THOUSANDS OF THEM. THEY'RE DRIVING ME MAD.
JODIE TALKS TO ME ALL THE TIME.
WHAT DOES HE SAY WHEN HE TALKS TO YOU?
HE TELLS ME ABOUT A LITTLE BOY WHO DIED IN MY ROOM. JODIE SAYS I'M GOING TO LIVE HERE FOREVER SO I CAN PLAY WITH THE BOY.
ONE NIGHT BEFORE SHE WENT TO BED, KATHY LOOKED IN THE MIRROR AND SAW HERSELF AS AN OLD WOMAN. SHE YELLED A BLOOD-CURDLING SCREAM.
NO! NO! THIS IS NOT HAPPENING TO ME. MAKE IT STOP!

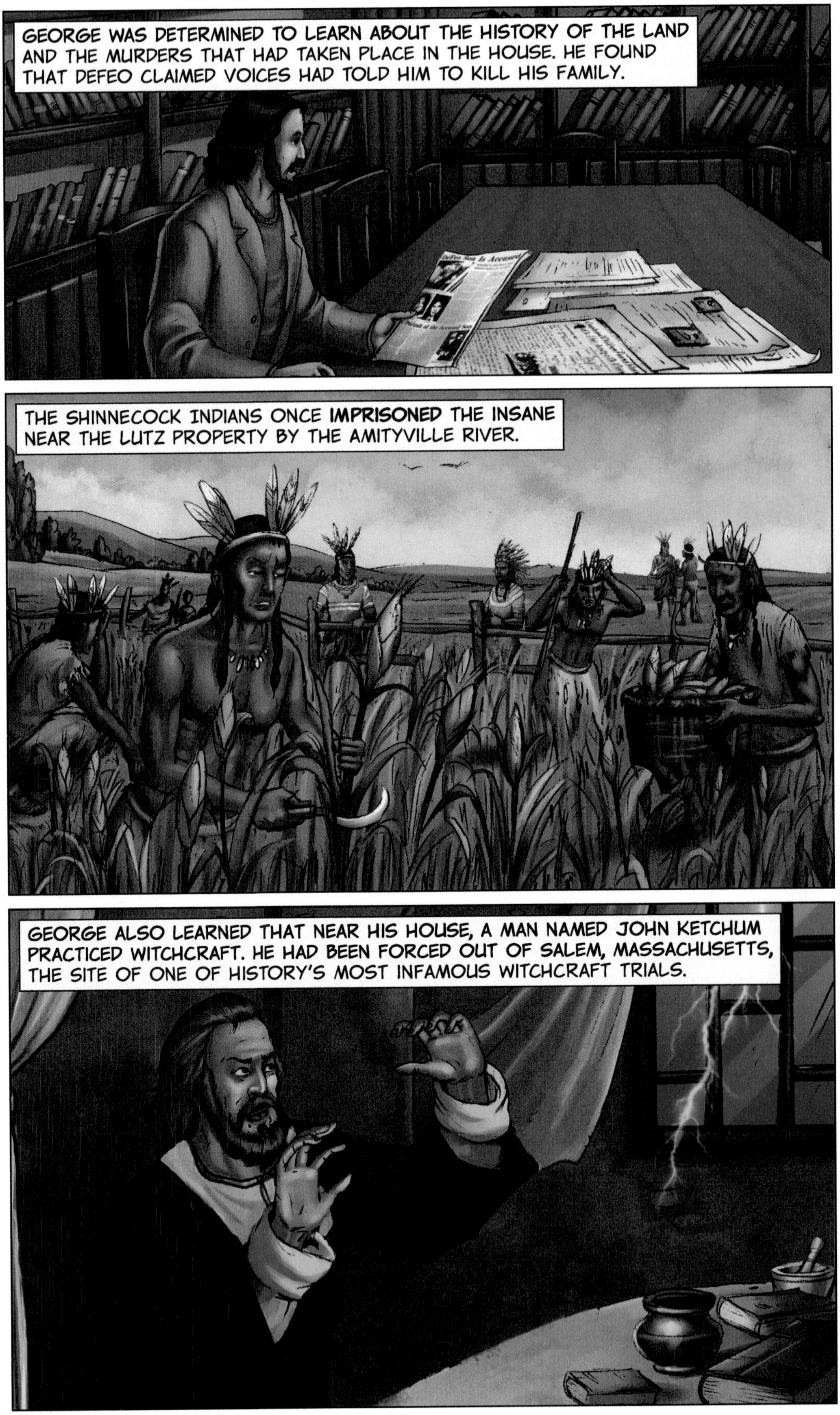
GEORGE WAS DETERMINED TO LEARN ABOUT THE HISTORY OF THE LAND AND THE MURDERS THAT HAD TAKEN PLACE IN THE HOUSE. HE FOUND THAT DEFEO CLAIMED VOICES HAD TOLD HIM TO KILL HIS FAMILY.
DeFeo Son Is Accused
THE SHINNECOCK INDIANS ONCE **IMPRISONED** THE INSANE NEAR THE LUTZ PROPERTY BY THE AMITYVILLE RIVER.
GEORGE ALSO LEARNED THAT NEAR HIS HOUSE, A MAN NAMED JOHN KETCHUM PRACTICED WITCHCRAFT. HE HAD BEEN FORCED OUT OF SALEM, MASSACHUSETTS, THE SITE OF ONE OF HISTORY'S MOST INFAMOUS WITCHCRAFT TRIALS.

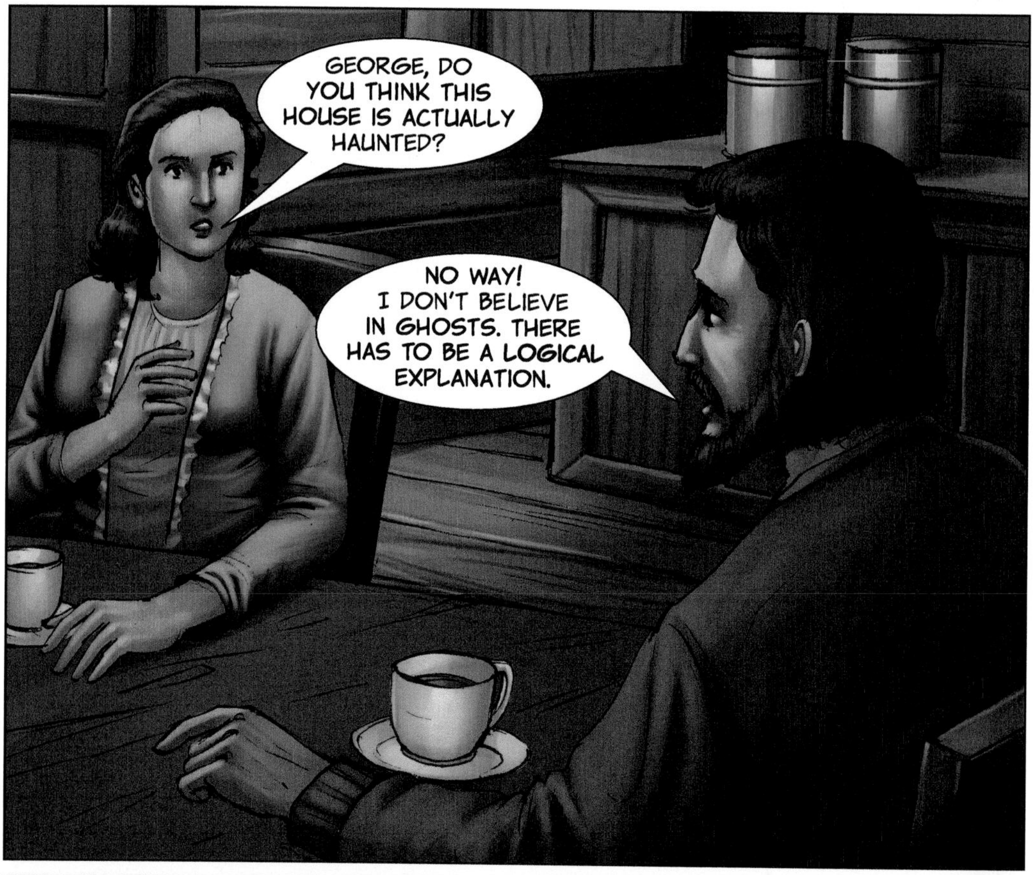
GEORGE, DO YOU THINK THIS HOUSE IS ACTUALLY HAUNTED?
NO WAY! I DON'T BELIEVE IN GHOSTS. THERE HAS TO BE A LOGICAL EXPLANATION.

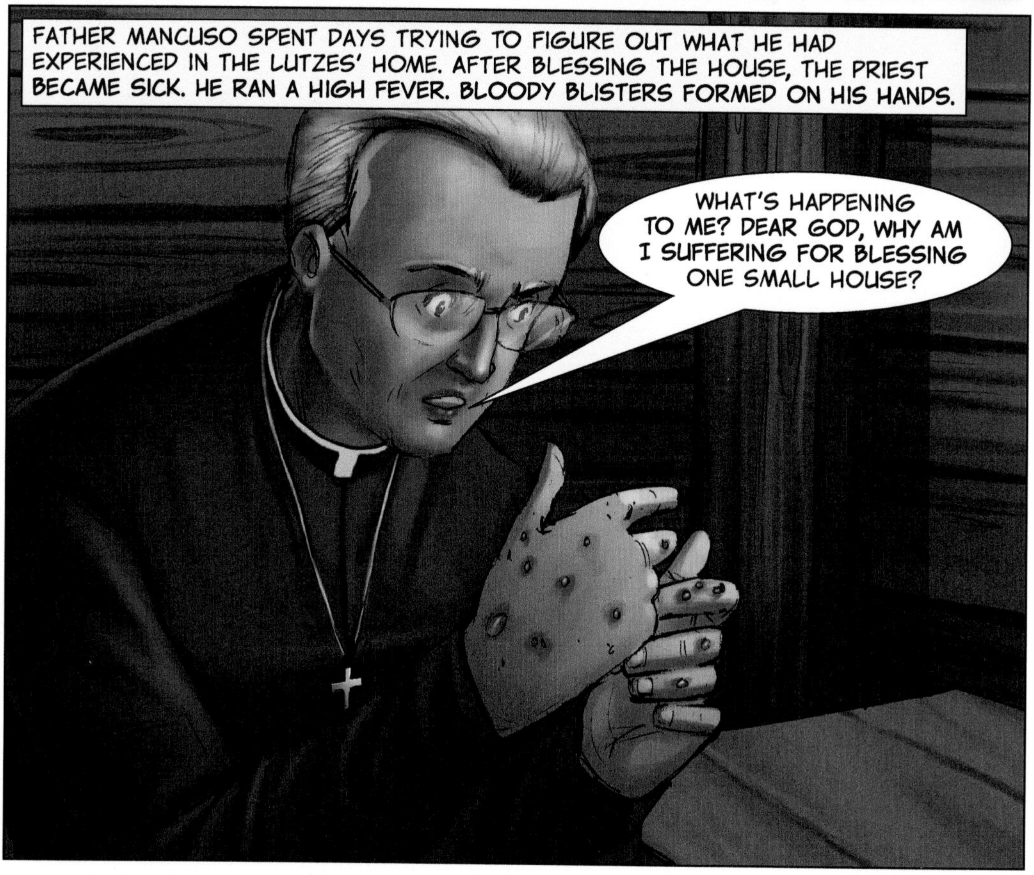
FATHER MANCUSO SPENT DAYS TRYING TO FIGURE OUT WHAT HE HAD EXPERIENCED IN THE LUTZES' HOME. AFTER BLESSING THE HOUSE, THE PRIEST BECAME SICK. HE RAN A HIGH FEVER. BLOODY BLISTERS FORMED ON HIS HANDS.
WHAT'S HAPPENING TO ME? DEAR GOD, WHY AM I SUFFERING FOR BLESSING ONE SMALL HOUSE?

EARLY IN THE MORNING ON JANUARY 14, GEORGE LISTENED AS A MARCHING BAND PLAYED EAR-SHATTERING MUSIC.

MOMENTS LATER, A MENACING FIGURE HOVERED OVER CHRIS AS HE LAY IN BED. GEORGE TRIED TO RUSH TO HIS SON'S SIDE, BUT SOMETHING WAS HOLDING HIM BACK.

IT'S IN CHRIS'S ROOM. IT'S GOT HIM!

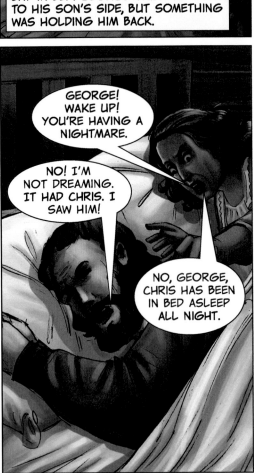

GEORGE! WAKE UP! YOU'RE HAVING A NIGHTMARE.

NO! I'M NOT DREAMING. IT HAD CHRIS. I SAW HIM!

NO, GEORGE, CHRIS HAS BEEN IN BED ASLEEP ALL NIGHT.

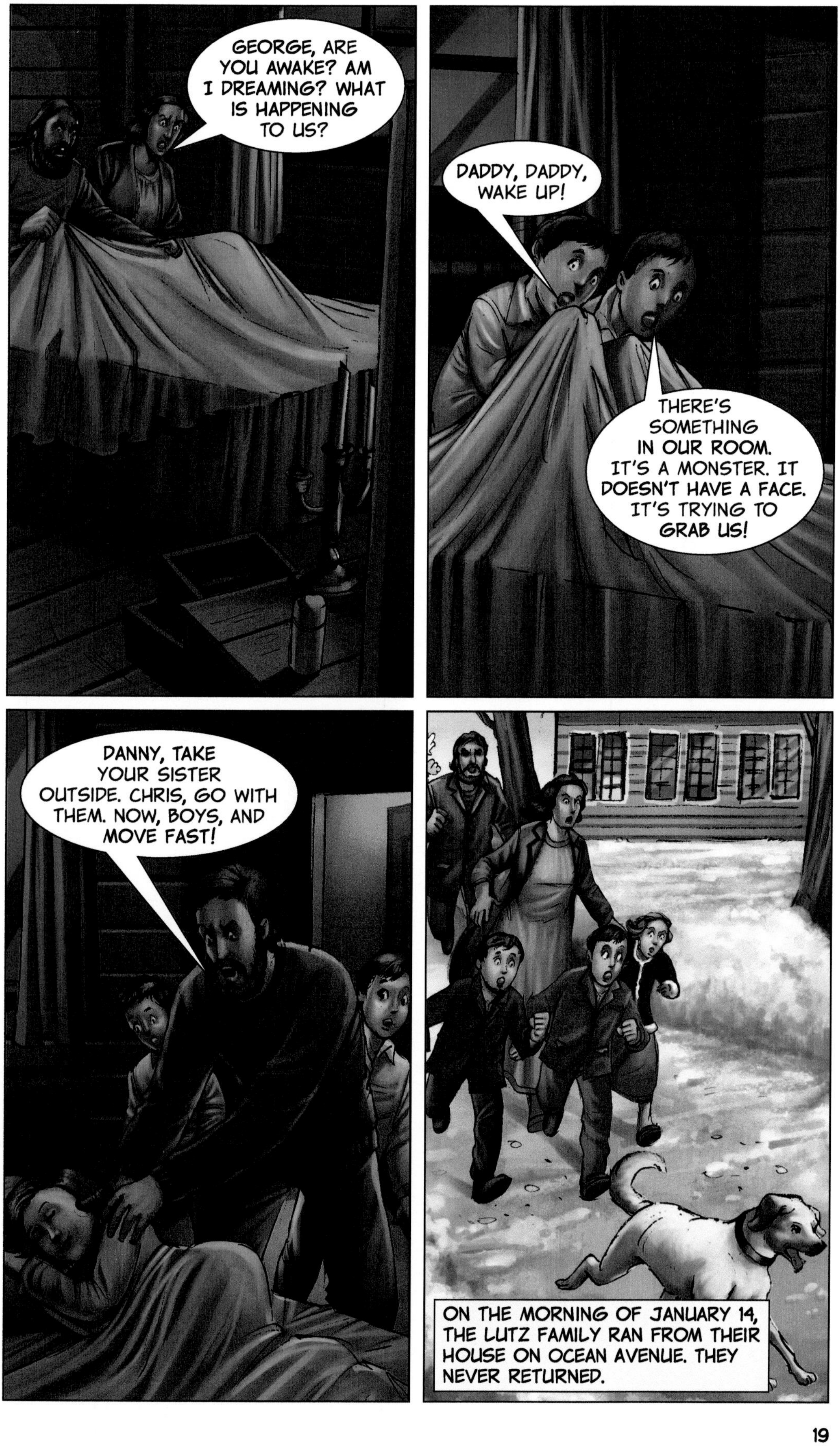
GEORGE, ARE YOU AWAKE? AM I DREAMING? WHAT IS HAPPENING TO US?
DADDY, DADDY, WAKE UP!
THERE'S SOMETHING IN OUR ROOM. IT'S A MONSTER. IT DOESN'T HAVE A FACE. IT'S TRYING TO GRAB US!
DANNY, TAKE YOUR SISTER OUTSIDE. CHRIS, GO WITH THEM. NOW, BOYS, AND MOVE FAST!
ON THE MORNING OF JANUARY 14, THE LUTZ FAMILY RAN FROM THEIR HOUSE ON OCEAN AVENUE. THEY NEVER RETURNED.

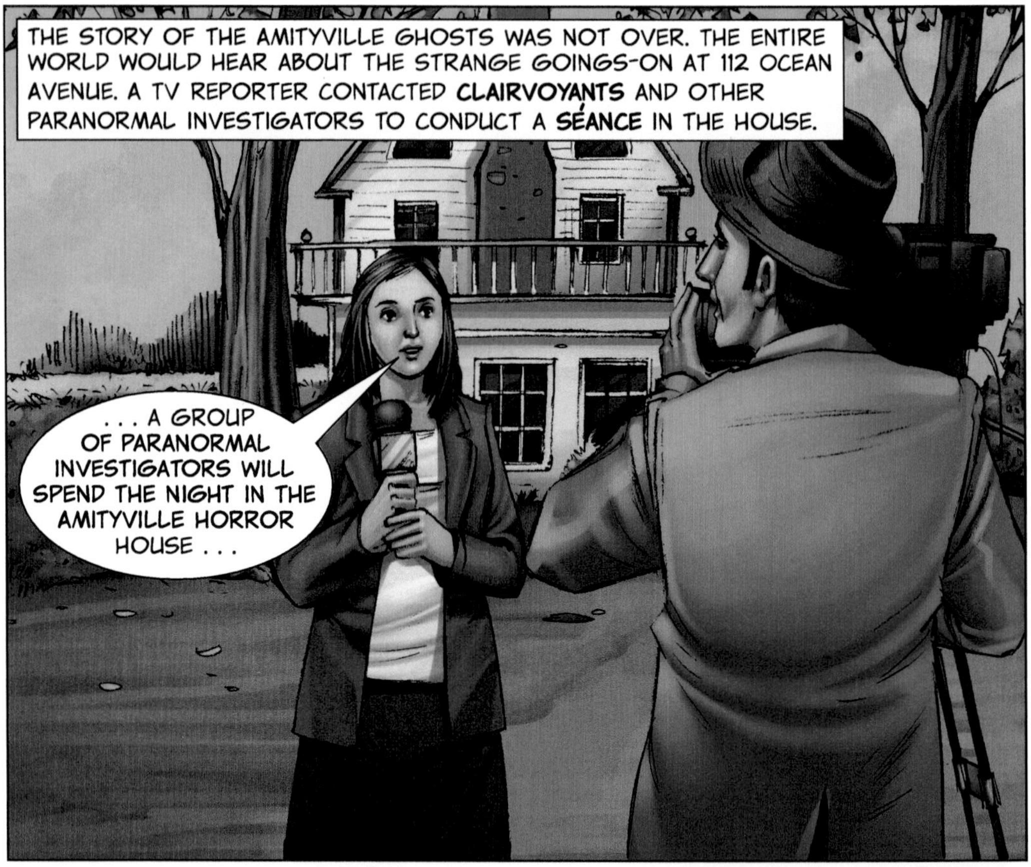
THE STORY OF THE AMITYVILLE GHOSTS WAS NOT OVER. THE ENTIRE WORLD WOULD HEAR ABOUT THE STRANGE GOINGS-ON AT 112 OCEAN AVENUE. A TV REPORTER CONTACTED **CLAIRVOYANTS** AND OTHER PARANORMAL INVESTIGATORS TO CONDUCT A **SÉANCE** IN THE HOUSE.
. . . A GROUP OF PARANORMAL INVESTIGATORS WILL SPEND THE NIGHT IN THE AMITYVILLE HORROR HOUSE . . .

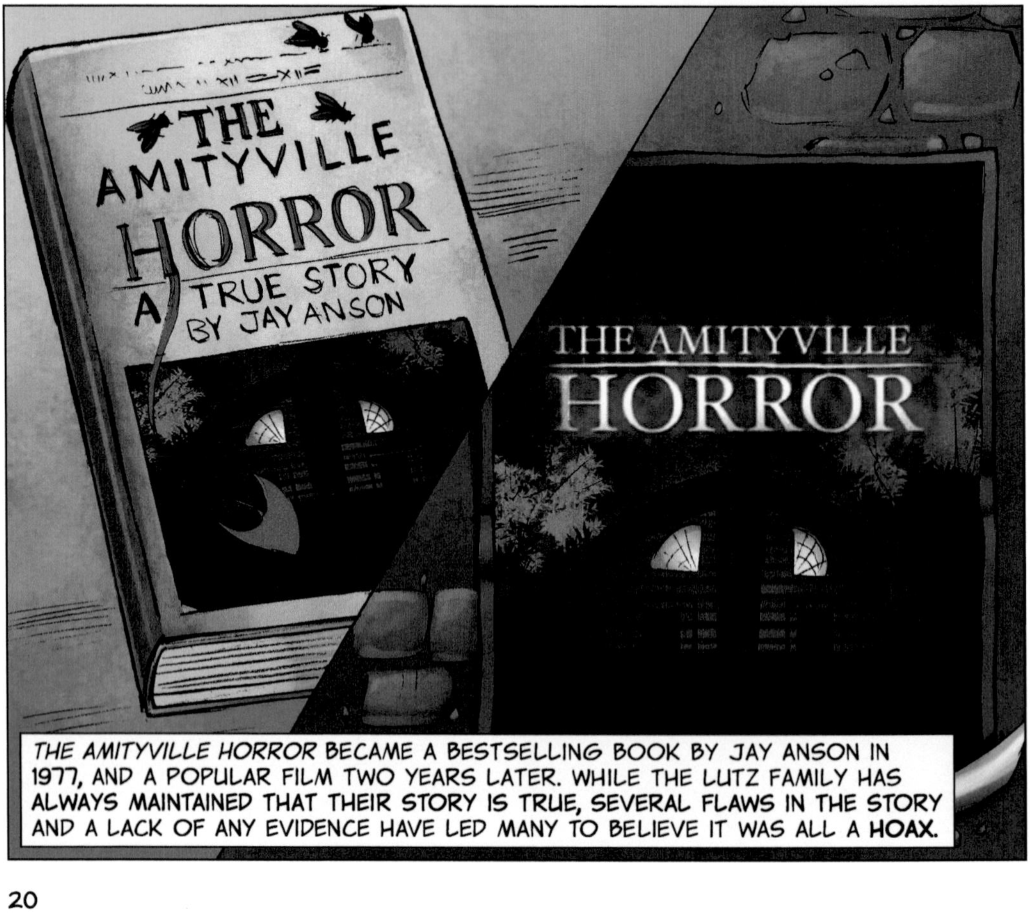
THE AMITYVILLE HORROR
A TRUE STORY
BY JAY ANSON
THE AMITYVILLE HORROR
THE AMITYVILLE HORROR BECAME A BESTSELLING BOOK BY JAY ANSON IN 1977, AND A POPULAR FILM TWO YEARS LATER. WHILE THE LUTZ FAMILY HAS ALWAYS MAINTAINED THAT THEIR STORY IS TRUE, SEVERAL FLAWS IN THE STORY AND A LACK OF ANY EVIDENCE HAVE LED MANY TO BELIEVE IT WAS ALL A **HOAX**.

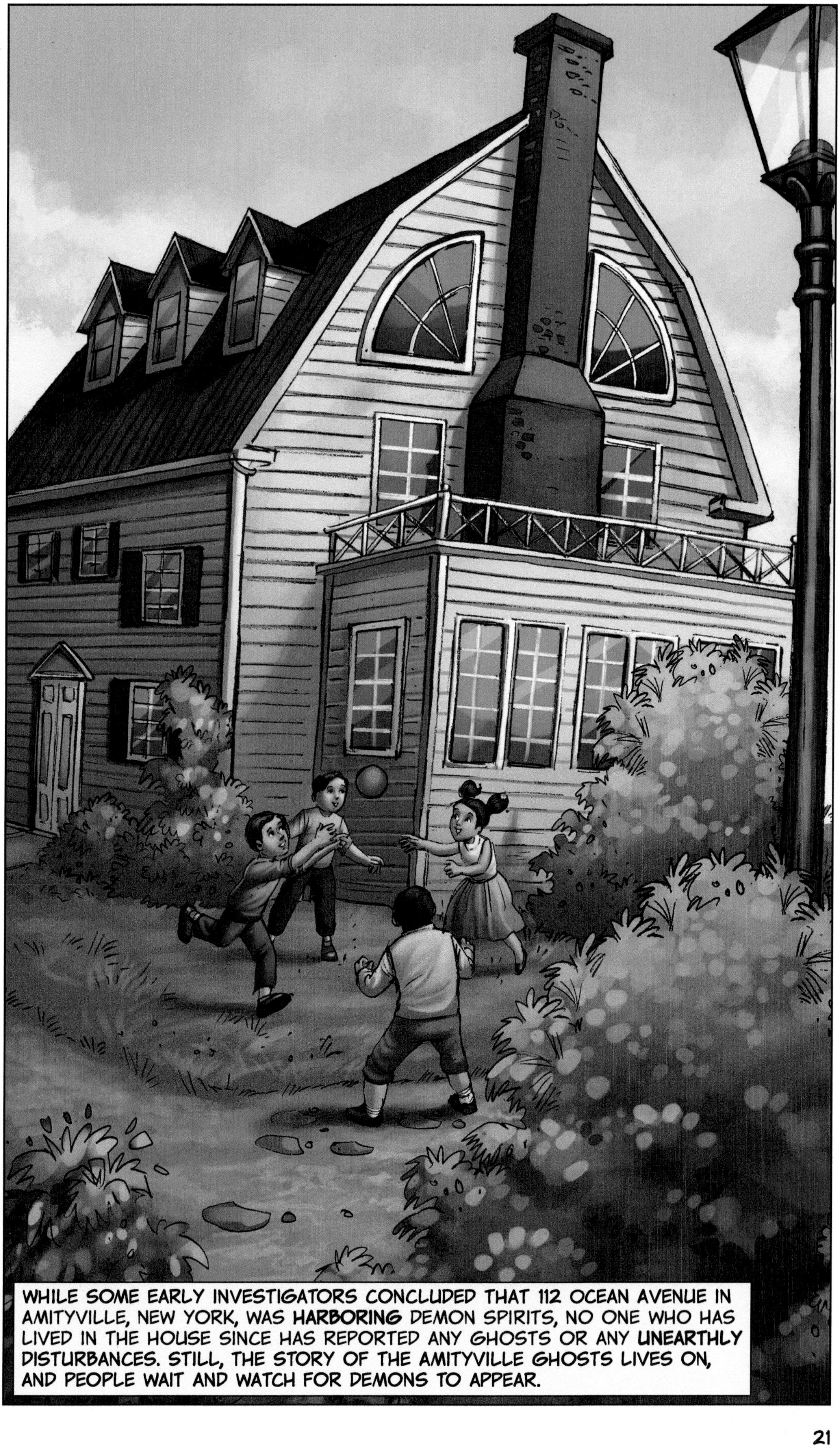
WHILE SOME EARLY INVESTIGATORS CONCLUDED THAT 112 OCEAN AVENUE IN AMITYVILLE, NEW YORK, WAS **HARBORING** DEMON SPIRITS, NO ONE WHO HAS LIVED IN THE HOUSE SINCE HAS REPORTED ANY GHOSTS OR ANY **UNEARTHLY** DISTURBANCES. STILL, THE STORY OF THE AMITYVILLE GHOSTS LIVES ON, AND PEOPLE WAIT AND WATCH FOR DEMONS TO APPEAR.

More on Haunted Houses

- **Beardslee Castle**
Now a restaurant located in Little Falls, New York, Beardslee Castle's history is tainted with death and misfortune. The castle was built in 1860 and is located about 1 mile (2 km) from the Mohawk River. One of the oldest stories of the site comes from the 1700s, when a fortified homestead stood on the land. Two Native Americans are said to have found a store of ammunition in a tunnel beneath the buildings on the property. According to legend, the men died when the torches they were carrying ignited the ammunition they were trying to steal. Another story is about Abigail, a young maiden who died in the castle the night before her wedding. Her ghost is said to wear a white, high-collared gown, a wedding gown perhaps. Some also suspect that Anton "Pop" Christenson, a sickly gentleman who hanged himself in the manor, haunts the restaurant. Moreover, there was a series of fires, and a ghostly lantern allegedly blinded drivers and caused accidents, some of which were fatal, on nearby Route 5. As for the restaurant's employees, they have reported mysteriously overturned tables and chairs, flying silverware, unintelligible voices, howls, and screams.

- **Whaley House**
Located in Old Town San Diego, the Whaley House was at various times a courthouse, theater, billiard hall, and school. Many people now claim that Whaley House is the most haunted dwelling in America. One of the ghosts who supposedly haunts the house is Yankee Jim, also known as Santiago Robinson. In 1852, a jury convicted Yankee Jim of grand larceny. He was hanged off the back of a wagon where the house now sits, swinging "back and forth like a pendulum until he strangled to death." Attending the execution was Thomas Whaley, who bought the property a few years later and built a house on the land. After moving in, the Whaley family began hearing strange footsteps upstairs, as though a large man were stomping about. They said it was Yankee Jim. Thomas Whaley and his wife, Anna, never moved out of the house. People have seen the ghost of Thomas wearing a frock coat. Anna's spirit seems to drift about, usually downstairs. Other ghosts are said to include a long-haired girl, a playmate of the Whaley children who accidentally broke her neck in the backyard after running into a clothesline; Thomas Whaley Jr., who at 17 months old died in the upstairs bedroom; a little girl who drank some poison in the Whaley House kitchen; and a spotted dog.

Glossary

amiss (uh-MIS) Wrong or imperfect.

clairvoyants (kler-VOY-unts) People who can see or know things that they did not see happen or should know about.

embracing (im-BRAYS-ing) Holding someone in your arms or hugging.

entity (EN-tuh-tee) A being that exists or is thought to exist.

grisly (GRIZ-lee) Horrible and causing fear.

harboring (HAR-bor-ing) Holding, containing, or providing someone with shelter.

hoax (HOHKS) Something that has been faked.

imprisoned (im-PRIH-zund) Locked away in jail or in a prison.

logical (LO-jih-kul) Having clear thought based on facts; sensible.

maintained (mayn-TAYND) Believed or stated repeatedly that something was true.

motivated (MOH-tih-vay-ted) Eager or willing to make a deal.

paranormal (pa-ruh-NOR-mul) Not able to be explained by science.

séance (SAY-ahnts) A meeting at which people try to communicate with the spirits of dead people.

sensation (sen-SAY-shun) A particular feeling that the body experiences.

swarms (SWORMZ) Large numbers of insects, often in motion.

unearthly (un-ERTH-lee) Strange, unnatural, frightening, or not of this world.

Index

Websites

Due to the changing nature of Internet links, PowerKids Press has developed an online list of websites related to the subject of this book. This site is updated regularly. Please use this link to access the list:

www.powerkidslinks.com/jggs/amity/